JUNE 2010

NATIONAL INSTITUTE OF JUSTICE

RESEARCH
IN BRIEF

I0428519

Cost-Benefit Analysis

A GUIDE FOR DRUG COURTS AND OTHER CRIMINAL JUSTICE PROGRAMS

BY P. MITCHELL DOWNEY AND JOHN K. ROMAN

NCJ 246769

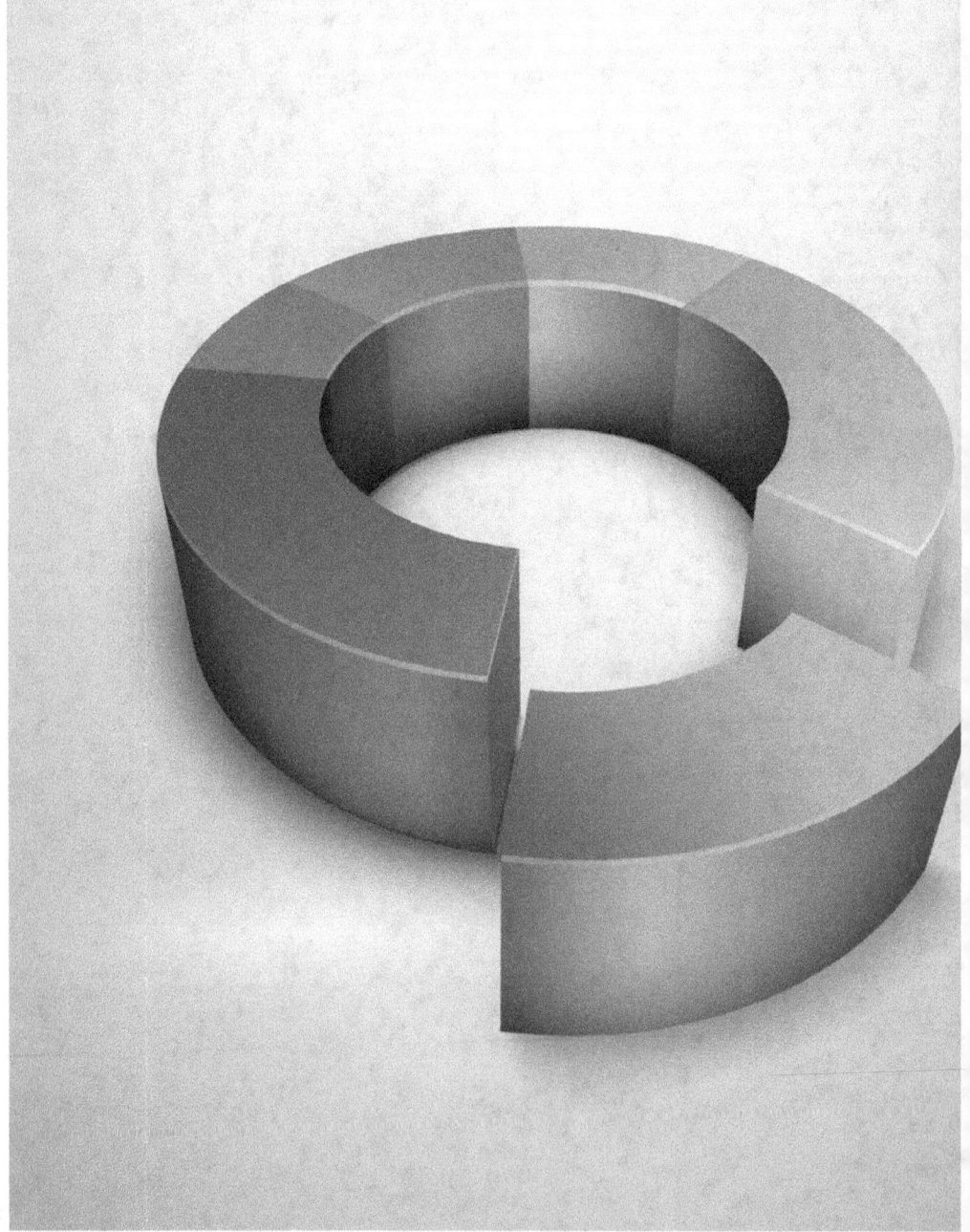

Cost-Benefit Analysis

A GUIDE FOR DRUG COURTS AND OTHER CRIMINAL JUSTICE PROGRAMS

BY P. MITCHELL DOWNEY AND JOHN K. ROMAN

Policymakers and practitioners face difficult decisions when they allocate resources. As resource constraints have tightened, the role of researchers in informing evidence-based and cost-effective decisions about the use of funds, labor, materials and equipment — and even the skills of workers — has increased. We believe research that can inform decisions about resource allocation will be a central focus of criminal justice research in the years to come, with cost-benefit analysis (CBA) among the key tools. This report about the use of CBA is aimed at not only researchers but also practitioners and policymakers who use research to make choices about how to use limited resources. Although we include NIJ's Multi-site Adult Drug Court Evaluation (MADCE) as an example of CBA in practice, this report is not just about using CBA in drug courts.

Our intent is to help researchers, state agencies, policymakers, program managers and other criminal justice stakeholders understand:

- What CBA is and in which contexts it is appropriate.

- Which kinds of information can — and should — be collected to facilitate a CBA.

- What the results of a CBA mean.

This report is divided into three sections. In the first section, "The Basics of Cost-Benefit Analysis," we describe the foundations of CBA: the motivation for performing a CBA, what CBA can (and cannot) tell us, and the general principles used in conducting CBA in terms of the conceptual basis and an applied framework. In the second section, "Cost-Benefit Analysis in Action: NIJ's MADCE," we apply the framework and illustrate the necessary steps using NIJ's MADCE as a case study. In the third section, "NIJ's MADCE Results," we present the findings from NIJ's MADCE and demonstrate how the results provide new and useful information that would not have been available without conducting such an analysis.

Report Highlights

In this report, we address several key cost-benefit analysis (CBA) concepts, including:

- The difference between what cost-benefit researchers believe they are producing and what policymakers often believe they are receiving. Researchers believe they are estimating societal benefits, whereas policymakers believe they are receiving estimated fiscal benefits; this confusion has important policy implications (see "Cost-benefit analysis: What and why" on page 5).

- A variety of data sources and analytical approaches that have wide applicability throughout criminal justice CBA (see "Site-specific prices" on page 16 and "National prices" on page 17).

- Practical considerations for conducting a CBA and a look at information often missing from technical reports, which tend to focus more on principles and theoretical foundations (see sidebar, "Practical Considerations of Conducting a Cost-Benefit Analysis," on page 20).

The Basics of Cost-Benefit Analysis

Cost-benefit analysis: What and why. Why conduct a CBA? Unlike other types of analysis, CBA offers a comprehensive framework for combining a range of impacts. Consider a law that bans smoking in restaurants. Such a law has several positive effects (called benefits), including improved health of restaurant staff and diners as well as a more pleasant atmosphere for nonsmokers. The same law, however, also has some negative impacts (called costs), such as inconveniencing smokers and the added expense to restaurant owners to enforce and publicize the new law. Note that these impacts are not all financial. Although money is a useful metric for combining diverse outcomes, the key contribution of CBA is providing a framework on which to combine diverse impacts.

CBA is usually subject to two key criticisms. First, some people argue that CBA values things that cannot be valued, such as pain and suffering from violent victimization or loss of life. A common response to this criticism is to ask, "Would you support a program that spent $1 trillion to prevent a single homicide?" If you would not support such a program, then you are implicitly conducting a CBA and designating the value of a human life. In the same way, CBA seeks to balance the use of resources to solve a variety of problems, but to do so using evidence carefully, consistently and transparently.

The second criticism involves the way in which things are valued. For instance, CBA theory uses wages and earnings to approximate the value of someone's time and his or her productivity (see sidebar, "Considerations in Valuing Time"). Suppose a probation officer makes $25 per hour and a program saves him or her one hour. Standard CBA counts that one hour saved as a $25 benefit of the program. Many people find this approach inappropriate. The program may save one hour of "probation officer time," but this savings doesn't reduce agency costs. This issue highlights the importance of understanding CBA's goals: CBA does not seek to estimate fiscal savings but, rather, seeks to estimate social value. If that same probation officer spends his or her time doing another productive activity, as is assumed in CBA and economic theory, then this is a productivity gain and a benefit of the program. Still, it is reasonable (in our view) to criticize this assumption. This criticism, however, doesn't reject CBA in its entirety — rather, it is an argument about *how* CBA is conducted. A good CBA makes its assumptions transparent and identifies how these assumptions affect the results.

These arguments are not the only criticisms of CBA. Analysts often debate what discount rate to use, the validity of willingness-to-pay in the presence of inequality, and the difficulty in valuing equity and justice. In this report, we focus on the two criticisms initially described, because they are commonly heard and can be addressed through the practice of CBA.

CBA is inherently comparative; it is particularly useful for comparing two programs or alternatives that may have different types of impacts. When a program's net benefits are compared with zero (i.e., deemed "cost beneficial" or "not cost beneficial"), the net benefits are implicitly being compared with business as usual (i.e., what is usually done without the policy change).

CONSIDERATIONS IN VALUING TIME

A critical element of cost-benefit analysis (CBA) is valuing the time spent by workers. A program might increase a probationer's time spent with a probation officer, reducing the amount of time that the officer has to fulfill other responsibilities. It is possible that neither of these outcomes will have an impact on an agency's spending, but if the time could have been spent productively on other activities, then both outcomes have implications for available resources. In other words, without the program, the officer may have conducted additional patrols, thereby contributing to society. Spending time on additional patrols and community-based approaches to crime prevention contributes to the larger community. Without the program in place, the probation officer may instead spend time on enhanced client interactions that are designed to reduce violence and revocations. CBA draws upon a long tradition in economic theory and assumes that an individual's wage is equal to the marginal value contributed to society by his or her time. This assumption is an uncomfortable one for many people, including the authors of this report. However, this approach remains standard practice in the literature, and this report repeatedly uses wages to measure productivity and the social value of time.

What Cost-Benefit Analysis Can and Cannot Do

Cost-benefit analysis (CBA) can:

- Tell us the impact of a program on a wide range of outcomes.
- Offer guidance on how to balance these diverse impacts.
- Tell us how the program draws from (or contributes to) the pool of available resources.

CBA cannot:

- Provide the end-all, be-all, irrefutable, definitive answer to all policy questions.
- Do anything without a strong impact analysis.
- Tell us how much money an agency or jurisdiction will save by implementing a particular program.

CBA is useful because it combines different types of information into a single metric, allowing for comparisons that could not otherwise be made. CBA provides guidance on how to balance these different types of impacts. CBA also tells decision-makers how the program draws from or adds to resources (not just funding) that are available for other programs and offers guidance on what it would take to replenish those resources.

CBA, however, is not a magic bullet that can answer all policy questions. For one thing, without a strong impact evaluation, a CBA is meaningless; that is, **to estimate (and value) the impact of a program on resources, we need to be able to convincingly estimate what effect the program had** (i.e., compare outcomes when the program is present with outcomes when the program is absent). To do so requires implementing a strong research design (including, but not limited to, random assignment) and collecting enough data for *both* the treatment and comparison groups to determine what would have happened in the absence of the program. Because CBA is *inherently comparative,* data about program participants alone is not enough. Second, although CBA theory provides a framework for valuing any impact, as a matter of practice, impacts often simply can't be valued (see "Cost-Benefit Analysis in Action: NIJ's MADCE" on page 11).

Finally, CBA does not tell us how much money an agency or jurisdiction can expect to save from a particular program. This is not the purpose of a CBA, and the methods are not designed to answer this question. CBA, as described below, is about social well-being and resources, not about fiscal impacts. This is an important point that is often overlooked and must be considered. Within this report, we emphasize the discrepancy between what cost-benefit researchers think they are producing (i.e., estimates of societal well-being) and what policy stakeholders think they are receiving (i.e., advice about fiscal savings).

The steps of a cost-benefit analysis. CBA can be thought of as progressing through four steps:

1. Choose the population.

2. Select potential impacts.

3. Consider how the program might change well-being.

4. Determine how society values these changes.

It is important to keep in mind that the final goal of a CBA is to estimate the social benefit (or cost) of a program. In the following paragraphs, we describe the conceptual steps and then offer an applied framework. Finally, we show how these steps work in practice through NIJ's MADCE.

1. Choose the population. The first step of a CBA is to determine the population you are interested in (called the "standing" of the study). In brief, the study's standing is the group whose well-being is changed by a new policy or practice. Stated another way, the standing is the population whose costs and benefits are counted. A study's standing might be all of society, all of society excluding the program participants, or all tax-paying citizens. Choosing which group has standing is a value-based decision that depends on the nature of the program, the analysis, and the decision-makers or stakeholders. For example, a CBA of a mandatory job training program for recipients of government assistance generally includes program participants in its standing, whereas a CBA of sentencing policy generally does not include prisoners in its standing (although it could). In practice, the selection of the standing in the aforementioned examples means that one cost of the job training program would be the value of the time that clients give up to participate in training (economists call this the "opportunity cost" of participants' time), whereas a sentencing CBA would not include the opportunity cost of the prisoners' time.

2. Select potential impacts. Select the potential impacts to include in the analysis. First, consider what might have changed as a result of the program. In a criminal justice context, potential impacts often mean changes in behavior (e.g., employment, criminal offenses) or resources used (e.g., police time, jail beds, court hearings). Think about what effects the program may have had, identify the impacts you can plausibly measure, and estimate the size of the changes that the program caused (if any). This step is the reason that a CBA relies on a strong impact evaluation. Without an impact evaluation, estimating the program's effects is impossible, and, thus, there are no effects to value. Economists sometimes say that an evaluation is "well identified" if it convincingly isolates the causal impacts of the program.

3. Consider how the program might change well-being. Consider how the program's effects might have changed the well-being (either positively or negatively) of someone in the standing. For instance, a program that increases meetings with a probation officer might decrease the time that the officer has to work with other clients. A program that improves participants' educational outcomes might lead participants to make greater contributions to society through employment. Regardless, this step translates the program's impacts into social well-being.[1]

4. Determine how society values these changes. Find information either from within or outside of the evaluation to determine how society values these changes. For instance, ask, "How much does society value a probation officer's time?" Or, "How much does society value more and better education?" Keep in mind that the answers to these questions have nothing to do with the analysts' beliefs about how much these issues

---

[1] Economists usually call this "social welfare" or just "welfare." To avoid confusion with the unrelated government assistance programs, we often say "well-being" instead, even though researchers more commonly use the term "welfare."

should be valued; rather, the analyst must use existing data to estimate, based on observed behavior, how society does in fact value these changes.

Steps 3 and 4 could be considered the key contributions to — and the key challenges of — conducting a CBA.

Implementing the conceptual framework. To implement the conceptual framework, we must "ground" our thinking: First, we think of each cost (or benefit) as a price multiplied by a quantity. Because a cost is simply a negative benefit, we tend to use the terms "costs" and "benefits" interchangeably. Using the terms interchangeably allows us to illustrate that both costs and benefits measure how the program affected social well-being (either positively or negatively) and that costs and benefits are not fundamentally different concepts.

The quantities used in CBA are the main project inputs (e.g., hours of training) and the outcomes of interest (e.g., number of arrests, number of treatment episodes, hours of employment). These quantities are drawn from the impact analysis, which must include comparable information for the comparison group. The prices are the way that well-being is affected (e.g., resources used per arrest/treatment episode, social value contributed by employment). This information is drawn from surveys, observations, prior research and a variety of other sources of information. We discuss some examples in the next section.

After deciding which impacts to include, the researchers determine the measure (quantity) and value (price) of the impacts and then multiply the quantity (e.g., number of additional drug treatment episodes) by the price (e.g., cost of a drug treatment episode) to get the cost (e.g., additional drug treatment episodes). The researchers then can add together a range of different costs and benefits to create a measure of "net benefits." Net benefits refers to the benefits minus the costs. For instance, if a program costs $50 per participant but yields $150 in social welfare per participant, on average, then we say the program yields $100 in net benefits (per participant). The resulting net benefits yield an estimate of how participants improved or harmed society, combining an array of different types of impacts.

The key question is whether the net benefits to society are greater for the treatment group (i.e., program participants) than for the comparison group. If so, this finding suggests that the program improved societal well-being, either by reducing the harm that participants would have done to society without the program (i.e., decreasing costs) or by increasing the value of participants' societal contributions (i.e., increasing benefits). Because the researchers estimated the quantities using rigorous methods (as developed in the impact analysis), we have some confidence that the program itself caused the difference.

Cost-Benefit Analysis in Action: NIJ's MADCE

In this section, we illustrate the general principles previously described with a practical example, relying on the CBA component of NIJ's MADCE. We discuss the evaluation of the MADCE only briefly. For more information about NIJ's MADCE, readers may access NIJ's website, which includes links to a number of related publications (search NIJ.gov, keyword: MADCE).

In fiscal year 2003, NIJ awarded a grant to the Urban Institute for a multisite process, impact and cost evaluation of adult drug courts in partnership with the Center for Court Innovation and RTI International. The study included 23 drug courts in eight states, with the comparison group drawn from six comparison groups where drug court access was limited. Overall, 1,787 individuals participated in the study, with about two-thirds of them in the treatment group. Study participants were interviewed at the time they enrolled in drug court (or would have enrolled for the comparison group) and then were interviewed again both six months and 18 months later. At the 18-month interview, the study participants also received a drug test. Finally, at 24 months, the researchers collected official records describing participants' contact with the criminal justice system. The researchers also collected cost data from interviews, document review and direct observation of court practices. They analyzed the data using statistical procedures that accounted for differences between people based on a large list of personal characteristics and site-specific effects, thereby effectively isolating the impact of drug court participation on each individual's outcomes.

Figure 1. NIJ's Multi-site Adult Drug Court Evaluation Conceptual Framework

Drug Court Context	Target Population Severity	Drug Court Practices
Community Setting • Demographics • Urbanicity • Drug arrest rate • Poverty/economics **Drug Laws** • Mandatory sentences • Drug law severity **Court Characteristics** • Court size • Court resources	**Drug Use** • Addiction severity • Drugs of abuse • Drug use history **Criminality** • Felony/misdemeanor charge • Recidivism risk — prior arrests/convictions • Opportunity to offend (street days) **Other Risk Factors** • Health problems • Mental health problems • Employment problems • Housing instability • Family conflict • Family support • Close ties to drug users • Close ties to lawbreakers **Demographics** • Age, gender, race • Marital status, children • Education, income	**Use of Legal Pressure** • Severity of consequences for failure **Individual Court Experiences** • Drug court participation • Drug testing requirements, practices • Sanctions rules, practices • Supervision requirements/ practices • Prosecution involvement • Interactions with judge and supervising officers • Court appearances **Drug Court Practices** • Leverage • Program intensity • Predictability • Rehabilitation focus • Timeliness of intervention • Admission requirements • Completion requirements **Drug Treatment** • Treatment history • Days of treatment by type • Treatment requirements • Support services by type — offered and used

The conceptual framework for the MADCE shows how resources (called "inputs") are invested to create activities designed to produce program outputs. The framework proposes that program activities will result collectively in immediate or short-term outcomes for the participants. These immediate and short-term outcomes typically are measured while the participants are still in the program and include changes in perception and behavior, such as drug use and participation in treatment. Program participation also is expected to result in long-term outcomes, such as changes in drug use, criminal behavior and other functions. The framework controls for characteristics of the target population relating to drug use, criminality and other risk factors. The framework also recognizes external conditions beyond the program's control. These conditions relate to the general community, legal and penal codes, and the criminal court. NIJ's MADCE tested the impact of court-mandated treatment in a *drug court context*. The MADCE comparison groups are not "controls" that receive no treatment; some of the probationers receive court-ordered drug treatment, and other probationers use treatment alternatives for safe communities models.

Offender Perceptions	In-Program Behavior	Post-Program Outcomes
Perceived Legal Pressure • Severity and likelihood of termination and alternative sentence	**Compliance With Drug Intervention** • Likelihood of entry • Number and type of drug test violations • Percentage of treatment days attended • Treatment duration and retention • Treatment graduation and termination	**Reduced Drug Use** • Any, type, and frequency of self-reported use post-program • Results of saliva test
Motivations • Readiness to change stage		**Reduced Recidivism** • Any, type, and frequency of self-reported offending post-program • Any, type, and number of arrests/convictions post-program • Decrease in post-intervention incarceration
Understanding of Rules • Received expected sanctions and rewards • Understood expected behavior		
Perceived Risk of Sanctions and Rewards • General deterrence • Certainty/severity of sanctions • Certainty and value of rewards	**Compliance with Supervision** • Court FTAs — percentage of scheduled • Case management FTAs — percentage of scheduled • Violations of supervision requirements • Drug court graduation	**Improved Functioning** • Reduction in health and mental health problems • Increase in likelihood and days of employment • Gains in economic self-sufficiency • Reductions in family problems
Perceptions of Court Fairness • Procedural justice • Distributive justice • Personal involvement of judge and supervising officer		**Post-Program Use of Services** • Type and amount of drug treatment/aftercare • Type and amount of other support services

Defining impacts and estimating quantities. As discussed earlier, we began our analysis by **identifying our population of interest** (standing). In principle, the standing could include the program participants themselves. Based on prior research, however, we expected drug court to lead to a variety of quality-of-life improvements, such as less severe drug addiction or improved self-esteem. Estimating an individual's personal value from these benefits seemed difficult or impossible. To simplify the analysis, we excluded participants from our standing and valued only drug court's impacts on broader society. Note that societal benefits indirectly caused by reduced addiction (such as reduced criminal activity) or improved self-esteem (such as social benefits of employment) would still be valued. We simply excluded the direct benefits, which only the participants experienced.

Next, we sought to **define the impacts to be considered.** We asked the following questions: "Did the program participants come into contact with or directly affect society in some way? Did the program affect someone in a way that would not have otherwise happened? Did this impact require the use of some resources? Could this effect plausibly be valued?" Through these questions, we developed a list of potentially measurable drug court impacts (see Table 1, Outcomes Measured by NIJ's Multi-site Adult Drug Court Evaluation). Certainly, other impacts may exist,[ii] but we believe this list strikes a balance between comprehensiveness and feasibility.

Based on the impact evaluation designed as part of NIJ's larger MADCE effort, we then sought to **estimate the size of these impacts ("finding the quantities").** This step was straightforward, because a rigorous research design already had been developed and implemented for the impact analysis. We used two types of information: (a) the three in-depth interviews and (b) administrative records from state departments of corrections, the FBI and state data repositories. We estimated the impacts of drug court on arrests, incarcerations and criminal activity based on

---

[i] For instance, the interviewer also asked about needle use, which could have allowed us to estimate the impact of drug court on HIV/AIDS risk. However, after initially investigating this approach, we determined that making this additional calculation was unnecessarily complicated to estimate, and, therefore, we excluded it.

Table 1. Outcomes Measured by NIJ's Multi-site Adult Drug Court Evaluation

Category	Subcategory	Examples
Social productivity	Employment	Earnings
	Education	Schooling
	Services and support given	Child support payments, community service
	Monitoring	Probation officer time, drug tests, electronic monitor
Criminal justice system	Police	Arrests
	Courts	Hearings
	Corrections	Jail, prison (sanction or otherwise)
	Drug court	Case manager, administrative costs
Crime and victimization		Crimes committed*
Service use	Drug treatment	Emergency room, detoxification, residential care, outpatient, methadone
	Medical treatment	Hospital stays unrelated to drugs
	Mental health treatment	Stays in mental health facilities unrelated to drugs
	Other	Halfway houses, public housing, homeless shelters
Financial support use	Government	Welfare, disability, other entitlements
	Other	Money from family and friends

*Thirty-two subcategories of crime as defined by the National Incident-Based Reporting System.

administrative records, and we estimated the impacts of drug court on hearings, meetings, monitoring, treatment, and other services and support based on self-reported survey data.

Finally, we had to **value those impacts ("finding the prices").** We used two types of prices: (a) site-specific prices from the participating courts and (b) national data. Although we preferred site-specific data, often it wasn't possible to obtain separate prices for each site in the study. When site-specific data were not available, we relied on national price data. Because many of the data resources used in NIJ's MADCE have potential applications in a range of contexts, we discuss them in some detail here. However, this is a brief overview; interested readers should see the full report from the MADCE evaluation for a thorough discussion (see NCJRS.gov, keyword: 237112).

Site-specific prices

Prices of operating drug courts. In CBA, the first attempt to gather price information usually entails reaching out directly to the programs. In NIJ's MADCE, to determine the costs of operating drug courts (including, for example, regular hearings, meetings and drug tests), we conducted phone interviews with all 23 drug courts. We asked questions about the salaries of program staff and their level of involvement with the program, the costs of any outsourced treatment or drug testing, and the frequency and intensity of various activities. We complemented this survey with courtroom observation during site visits. Together, this information allowed us to translate the interview responses of program participants into specific values. For instance, we were able to convert interview data, such as "I was tested for drugs twice," into costs using the drug court's report of what types of drug testing it used, whether it outsourced those tests and how much it paid.

Prices of stays in homeless shelters. Sometimes a more involved or complicated approach is needed to estimate prices. Consider the price of stays in homeless shelters. In NIJ's MADCE, we relied on self-reported stays to estimate quantities, and we estimated the prices based on grant applications through the National Alliance to End Homelessness. These applications included the costs of operating a homeless shelter in a particular city. For cities that did not submit applications, we used publicly available data on house prices from the Department of Housing and Urban Development to find cities with similar housing costs. We assumed that the costs of homeless shelters in cities without applications were equal to costs in comparable cities with applications.

Prices of wages and salaries of key individuals in the criminal justice system. Some prices are relatively easy to come by using publicly available external data. For example, because NIJ's MADCE included so many jurisdictions and programs, key individuals (e.g., court personnel, law enforcement officers, treatment providers, probation officers) worked in too many different agencies for us to survey all of them. Instead, we estimated their wages and salaries using the Bureau of Labor Statistics' (BLS') Occupational Employment Statistics (OES). This publicly available information includes the average wages for very specific occupational categories for every metropolitan area in the country. We found that using the OES data, which is an accurate and easy-to-access source of information, was a more efficient approach than using widespread surveys.

Costs of incarceration. The final site-specific price we used was an estimate of the costs of incarceration. To estimate the costs of prison, we relied on the annual reports of state departments of corrections and followed an approach described in the Bureau of Justice Statistics (BJS) report *State Prison Expenditures, 2001.*[1] Essentially, the approach focuses on prison operating costs (excluding, for instance, land costs) and approximates the cost of an additional prisoner as the average operating cost of each prisoner. We took the same approach for jails. However, rather than obtaining annual reports for the large number of jails in the sample, we turned to BJS' *Census of Jail Facilities,* which contained the necessary information for all jails in the country.[2]

National prices

Site-specific prices are, in some ways, ideal for a CBA. These prices provide the jurisdictions being evaluated with the most accurate and relevant information for their costs and benefits of operation. However, if the target audience is a larger (e.g., national) array of stakeholders that are considering program implementation, you may want to consider basing estimates on national average prices, which can be useful. Moreover, in many domains, site-specific price information is not publicly available. As a result, researchers must rely on national information. In NIJ's MADCE, we used a variety of national data sources that included simple national averages, past-published analyses and our own analyses of national data.

Value of earnings and employment. For example, to estimate the value of earnings and employment when such data were missing in the interview, we relied on the BLS' Current Population Survey (CPS), the same data set on which monthly reports of the U.S. unemployment rate are based. The CPS asks thousands of respondents each month a variety of social and employment questions. We used characteristics such as age, race, education, gender and other established predictors to estimate what each program participant might be expected to earn in the labor market. This information allowed us to value contributions from employment when, for example, a participant reported being employed but did not report the wage.

Prices of drug treatment. The interview data also allowed us to measure the number of drug treatment episodes for a range of treatment types. We used averages drawn from the U.S. Department of Health and Human Services' Healthcare Cost and Utilization Project (HCUP) to estimate the costs of drug- or alcohol-related emergency room visits. The HCUP collects data from every hospital in the country and computes averages for specific types of visits (which also allowed us to use separate prices for participants of different ages). We also used the HCUP to estimate the costs of hospitalizations not related to drugs or alcohol. To estimate the costs of other types of drug treatment, we relied on the U.S. Substance Abuse and Mental Health Services Administration's Alcohol and Drug Services Study (ADSS).[3] ADSS surveyed hundreds of drug treatment providers in the United States (albeit nearly a decade ago) and estimated the costs of a variety of drug treatment modalities. Finally, because ADSS respondents do not include men and women living in prisons, we had to turn to an alternate source to estimate the costs of in-prison therapy. Here we used estimates from the CBA of Roebuck, French and McClellan.[4]

Prices of mental health treatment. Similar to determining the prices for drug treatment, we based many other national prices used in NIJ's MADCE on past-published cost-benefit studies. To estimate the price of residential mental health treatment, we used a large study published by the U.S. Department of Veterans Affairs (VA) that was based on cost analyses of services provided in its hospitals.[5] Although these data aren't likely to be representative of treatment facilities not associated with VA hospitals, the prices of mental health treatment are difficult to obtain, and approximations like these are sometimes necessary in CBA.

Costs of stays in halfway houses. To estimate the costs of stays in halfway houses, we relied on a study by Klein-Saffran.[6] For the costs of arrests, we based our estimates on a study by Cohen and colleagues.[7] Although these estimates are now quite dated, they are still the main source in most CBA studies, because replicating the studies would be very expensive. In practice, CBA often involves relying on older information updated for inflation.

Social costs of victimization. Estimates of the social costs of victimization (i.e., the financial and nonfinancial harm inflicted on victims by criminal activity) came from Roman's analysis of jury data, which is also commonly cited.[8] This example illustrates another core principle of CBA: When possible, it is generally preferred that prices be based on what economists call "revealed preferences," or behavior we actually observe in society (such as the harm that actual juries have associated with certain types of victimization), rather than estimates based on surveys of perceptions (in which respondents have little at stake and often aren't expected to provide reasonable answers). Of course, this isn't a completely settled matter,[9] but, as a rule of thumb, economists prefer revealed preferences.

In summary, we took a variety of approaches in estimating quantities (including surveys, interviews, courtroom observations and administrative data records) and prices (including peer-reviewed articles, published and unpublished evaluations, large-scale data collection efforts, and original analyses of individual-level data) (see sidebar, "Practical Considerations of Conducting a Cost-Benefit Analysis").

Combining prices and quantities to estimate net benefits

A common approach. When researchers estimate the actual net benefits of a program, they usually make separate estimates for each type of impact. For instance, when using a standard impact analysis, researchers might conclude that, on average, the program led to one additional

PRACTICAL CONSIDERATIONS OF CONDUCTING A COST-BENEFIT ANALYSIS

Key practical considerations in conducting a cost-benefit analysis (CBA) are as follows:

- **Make simplifying assumptions** based only on convenience and feasibility. For instance, NIJ's Multi-site Adult Drug Court Evaluation (MADCE) analysis excluded direct benefits to program participants, such as reduced addiction or improved self-esteem. We made this decision not on any principled theoretical grounds but rather because valuing direct benefits would be too difficult.

- **Use agency financial reports.** One common technique used in the MADCE analysis was using reports from state departments of corrections to estimate the costs of prison and similar information (which had already been gathered and aggregated) to estimate the costs of jails.

- **Substitute general data for specific data.** For instance, although the use of wages for drug court employees in the MADCE analysis would have been preferable, it also was impractical. Instead, the analysis relied on average wages of people within the same occupation. Similarly, the analysis often resorted to national data in the absence of city-level data.

- **Use older data.** For example, it is nearly universal in the literature to use estimates of the costs of arrest that are based on analyses of 20-year-old data.

- **Use data based on observed behavior if possible** rather than people's self-reported claims of how they would value something. For instance, to estimate the social costs of an assault, one may rely on (a) jury data reflecting court awards related to an assault or (b) surveys about how people think assaults should be valued. Although the literature includes some debate on this topic, the first approach is generally preferable.

- **Combine various data** from diverse sources. The prices gathered in NIJ's MADCE come from a range of sources, many of which may be useful in future criminal justice CBAs.

drug treatment episode and 0.5 fewer arrests. Then, with each impact separately estimated, the researchers value the estimated difference. Thus, in this example, if a treatment episode costs $100 and an arrest costs $300, on average, the program led to $100 in additional costs and $150 in benefits. The researchers then combine these two figures to estimate that the program had $50 in net benefits. In brief, it is standard to:

1. Estimate each impact,

2. Value each impact, and then

3. Combine the different impacts.

NIJ's approach in MADCE. We used a different approach than most researchers to estimate the actual net benefits of the program. First, we valued the domains listed in Table 1 (see page 15). We then combined the different activities within the same person. Suppose, for instance, that the comparison individual received three drug treatment episodes (each costing $100) and was arrested once (costing $300). We valued these events and combined them within the same person. Thus, we estimated that this individual had $600 of social costs ($100 for each of the three treatments and $300 for the arrest). If a treatment individual had five drug treatments and no arrests, we would estimate this individual had $500 of social costs ($100 for each treatment). With societal costs/benefits measured at the individual level, we can simply analyze this variable using the impact analysis approach developed for NIJ's main MADCE analyses. Because the treatment individual had $100 less in social costs than the comparison individual, we estimate that the program yielded $100 in net benefits. In other words, we conducted the following steps:

1. Valued the behaviors considered,

2. Combined the different behaviors, and then

3. Estimated the impact of the program.

The research community accepts both of these approaches. Each approach has the same steps (estimate the impacts, value them, aggregate them) but in a different order. Each approach also yields similar conclusions, but we believe that the second approach gives more accurate estimates of statistical significance. The debate, which centers on covariance between different types of effects, is somewhat technical, and we leave it for the research literature to determine. Our purpose in this section is to present a simple illustration of how analyses are conducted in CBA. In NIJ's MADCE, we used the prices previously discussed to value all of the domains listed in Table 1 (see page 15), then aggregated the results within each individual and estimated the program's impact using the statistical procedures briefly mentioned at the beginning of the next section, "NIJ's MADCE Results."

NIJ's MADCE Results

In this section, we present some main results from the cost-benefit portion of NIJ's MADCE. Our focus is on illustrating the types of conclusions to which CBA might lead, rather than on discussing the implications for drug courts. For more information and a discussion of policy implications, see the National Association of Drug Court Professionals' 2012 publication *What Have We Learned from the Multisite Adult Drug Court Evaluation? Implications for Practice and Policy.*[10]

As we discussed earlier, we valued a variety of domains and aggregated them for each individual to estimate that individual's impact on the well-being of society. We then used statistical procedures to estimate how program participation changed societal impacts. The main cost-benefit results are presented in Table 2, Net Benefits by Category for Drug Court Participants and Comparison Probationers.

The key conclusion from NIJ's MADCE is that the benefits from participating in drug court do not appear to exceed the costs of participating — that is, the net benefits do not differ significantly from the status quo. On the one hand, opponents reviewing this conclusion might think, "Drug courts are not cost-beneficial; they don't have positive net benefits." On the other hand, advocates might think, "Drug courts pay for themselves; the benefits cover the costs." Both views are accurate descriptions of the results, highlighting the importance of being able to understand and interpret the underlying study.

Readers should recall that CBA is naturally comparative and that when comparing the results to zero, we compare them to the status quo. If we believe that society places some inherent value on rehabilitation, then that isn't captured here, and drug courts are a way of expanding rehabilitation without the cost of losing social welfare. If we believe that society places some inherent value on being tough on crime, that perception also isn't captured here, and drug courts weaken that position without providing the social welfare benefits to justify such a stance.

Regardless of these headline findings, we can look beyond them to better explore the value of CBA. **The results illustrate the unique ability of CBA to balance different types of impacts.** The key insights of Table 2 are that the dominant cost of drug courts is drug treatment

Table 2. Net Benefits by Category for Drug Court Participants and Comparison Probationers

Category	Hierarchical Results (over the full follow-up)		
	Drug Court Participants	Comparison Probationers	Net Benefit
Social productivity	$20,355	$18,361	$1,994
Criminal justice system	− $4,869	− $5,863	$994
Crime and victimization*	− $6,665	− $18,231	$11,566
Service use*	− $15,326	− $7,191	− $8,135
Financial support use	− $4,579	− $3,744	− $835
Total	− $11,206	− $16,886	$5,680

*Difference is statistically significant ($p < 0.01$).

and that the dominant benefit is reduced crime/victimization. Although it's true that drug courts seemed to improve employment outcomes and save the justice system money by reducing arrests and incarcerations, these benefits pale in comparison with the benefits of averted victimizations. Similarly, although drug courts carry some processing costs (e.g., additional hearings, meetings with probation officers, carrying out administrative responsibilities), these costs are small compared with the costs of drug treatment. CBA has enabled us to narrow our focus by offering some guidance on how significant some of these gains (i.e., benefits) or losses (i.e., costs) are. The CBA implies that drug courts can be motivated primarily by crime reduction and that the key concern is treatment costs.

Finally, a key implication of the CBA results is that drug courts are doing exactly what they are supposed to do. Drug courts raised the costs of government financial support by connecting clients to government assistance programs for which they were qualified. Drug courts dramatically increased supervision costs because the drug courts involve so many additional meetings with probation officers and case managers. Drug courts increased treatment costs because clients are much more likely to receive drug treatment and receive it in greater intensity. These are the intended functions of drug courts, and they seem to be achieving these procedural goals well.

Concluding Thoughts

In this report, we have sought to illustrate what we view as the key theoretical and practical issues in conducting a CBA. We believe that CBA can be a useful research tool in the coming years because it offers a comprehensive framework for combining a range of impacts.

Throughout this report, we have strived to bridge the gap between how researchers and policymakers and other criminal justice stakeholders interpret CBA and to make it clear that CBA is about social well-being and resources, not about fiscal impacts. Although we think of a cost (or benefit) as a price multiplied by a quantity, these prices are not transaction prices (such as the price of groceries at the store) but, rather, the value of a particular outcome or action in society. We have provided a conceptual framework and an applied process (see "The Basics of Cost-Benefit Analysis" on page 5), illustrated these with an example (see "Cost-Benefit Analysis in Action: NIJ's MADCE" on page 11), and noted some common challenges and realities that are faced in conducting a CBA (see "What Cost-Benefit Analysis Can and Cannot Do" on page 7). We have acknowledged that CBA is not a magic bullet that can answer all policy questions, and we have touched on some of its key limitations. We repeat that a good CBA makes its assumptions transparent and determines how sensitive the results are to those assumptions.

Finally, we want to reemphasize the point that CBA is only one element of the research portfolio, and it can say nothing without a strong impact evaluation. In other words, data about program participants alone are insufficient for a CBA, and researchers must use rigorous research designs to develop and follow a comparison group.

In this report, we have focused on providing the reader with the tools to interpret CBAs appropriately and use them responsibly in making decisions. Although no analysis will be perfect, a good CBA can serve as a critical pillar of policy debate and can inform decisions responsibly.

Notes

1. Stephan, James J., *State Prison Expenditures, 2001,* Bureau of Justice Statistics Special Report, Washington, D.C.: U.S. Department of Justice, Office of Justice Programs, June 2004, NCJ 202949, http://www.bjs.gov/content/pub/pdf/spe01.pdf.

2. Stephan, James, and Georgette Walsh, *Census of Jail Facilities, 2006,* Washington, D.C.: U.S. Department of Justice, Office of Justice Programs, Bureau of Justice Statistics, December 2011, NCJ 230188, http://www.bjs.gov/content/pub/pdf/cjf06.pdf.

3. Substance Abuse and Mental Health Services Administration, *The ADSS Cost Study: Costs of Substance Abuse Treatment in the Specialty Sector,* Rockville, Md.: Substance Abuse and Mental Health Services Administration, Office of Applied Studies, 2003, http://samhsa.gov/data/adss/ADSSCostStudy.pdf.

4. Roebuck, M. Christopher, Michael T. French, and A. Thomas McClellan, "DATStats: Results from 85 Studies Using the Drug Abuse Treatment Cost Analysis Program (DATCAP)," *Journal of Substance Abuse Treatment* 25 (2003): 51-57.

5. Barnett, Paul G., and Magda Berger, "Indirect Costs of Specialized VA Inpatient Mental Health Treatment," Technical Report No. 6, U.S. Department of Veterans Affairs, Menlo Park, Ca.: Health Economics Resource Center, April 2003.

6. Klein-Saffran, Jody. "Electronic Monitoring vs. Halfway Houses: A Study of Federal Offenders." *Alternatives to Incarceration* (Fall 1995): 24-28, http://www.bop.gov/resources/research_projects/published_reports/gen_program_eval/orepralternatives.pdf.

7. Cohen, Mark A., Ted R. Miller, and Shelli B. Rossman, "The Costs and Consequences of Violent Behavior in the United States," in ed. National Research Council, *Understanding and Preventing Violence, Volume 4: Consequences and Control,* Washington, D.C.: National Academies Press, 1994: 67-166.

8. Roman, Jonathan Kilbourn, "What Is the Price of Crime? New Estimates of the Cost of Criminal Victimization," Dissertation, University of Maryland, College Park, 2009. Available through UMD Theses and Dissertations, http://hdl.handle.net/1903/9868.

9. Cohen, Mark A., Roland T. Rust, Sara Steen, and Simon T. Tidd, "Willingness-to-Pay for Crime Control Programs," *Criminology* 42 (February 2004): 89-110.

10. Rossman, Shelli B., and Janine M. Zweig, *What Have We Learned from the Multisite Adult Drug Court Evaluation? Implications for Practice and Policy,* Alexandria, Va.: National Association of Drug Court Professionals, 2012, http://www.nadcp.org/sites/default/files/nadcp/Multisite%20Adult%20Drug%20Court%20Evaluation%20-%20NADCP.pdf.

About the Authors

Mitch Downey is currently pursuing a Ph.D. in economics at the University of California, San Diego.

John K. Roman is a senior fellow in the Justice Policy Center at the Urban Institute.

For more information on analyzing the costs and benefits of crime interventions, see John Roman's *NIJ Journal* article, "Cost-Benefit Analysis of Criminal Justice Reforms," at http://nij.gov/journals/272/Pages/cost-benefit.aspx.

The National Institute of Justice is the research, development and evaluation agency of the U.S. Department of Justice. NIJ's mission is to advance scientific research, development and evaluation to enhance the administration of justice and public safety.

The National Institute of Justice is a component of the Office of Justice Programs, which also includes the Bureau of Justice Assistance; the Bureau of Justice Statistics; the Office for Victims of Crime; the Office of Juvenile Justice and Delinquency Prevention; and the Office of Sex Offender Sentencing, Monitoring, Apprehending, Registering, and Tracking (SMART).